First published in North America in 2007 by
Two-Can Publishing
11571 K-Tel Drive
Minnetonka, MN 55343
www.two-canpublishing.com

Edited by Jill Anderson
Cover design and illustration by Brad Norr Design
Illustrated by Vincent Boyer, Charles Dutertre, and Julien Norwood

Originally published in France by Tourbillon S.A.R.L. under the title *Les dessous des requins.*
Copyright © 2006 Tourbillon et Muséum national d'Histoire naturelle, Paris, France

Library of Congress Cataloging-in-Publication Data

Vadon, Catherine.
[Dessous des requins. English]
Meet the shark / by Catherine Vadon.
p. cm.
Summary: "Sharks are not the blood-thirsty, human-eating beasts people used to think they were.
This book explains the truth behind sharks' nasty reputation and explains what biologists now know about
the anatomy, behavior and life cycle of the majestic group of fish we call sharks"—Provided by publisher.
Includes bibliographical references.
ISBN 978-1-58728-598-1 (hardcover)
1. Sharks—Juvenile literature.  I. Title.
QL638.9.V3313 2007
597.3—dc22                    2007001073

1 2 3 4 5 6 / 12 11 10 09 08 07

Printed in France by Pollina - n° L42562-C

Photo and Illustration Credits:  pp. 8–9: barrier shark © Mark Spencer/Auscape/PHONE. p. 10 left: *Petit Parisien* back-cover, April 25th 1909
Collection Kharbine-Tapabor.  p. 11 top left: illus. by Alphonse de Neuville from *Vingt mille lieues sous les mers*, Jules Verne, Hetzel Ed., 1870
© Collection Kharbine-Tapabor; lower left: *L'Intrépide* cover, April 1st 1923, DR; lower right: *Jaws*, courtesy of Universal Studios LLLP. p.12 right:
hammerhead shark, Marcus Elieser Bloch, *Les Poissons* © Bibliothèque municipale de l'Image. p. 13 top left: requiem shark, César de Rochefort,
*Histoire naturelle et morale des Antilles de l'Amérique* © Bibliothèque centrale/MNHN; p. 13 center: thresher shark, Abbé Joseph Bonnaterre,
*Tableau encyclopédique et méthodique des trois règles de la nature: ichtyologie* © Bibliothèque centrale/MNHN. p. 15 left margin: © Musée du
quai Branly. p. 24 center: requiem shark and pilot fishes © Agence Images/Iconos; lower left: barrier shark and remoras © Tom Campbell/Still
pictures/BIOS. p. 25 top right: manta ray © Cartwright Ian/Age/Hoa-Qui; bottom: chimaera © Florian Graner/Nature PL/ Jacana. p. 27 top left:
scalloped hammerhead © Phillip Coller/PHONE; right: basking shark © Agence Images/Iconos. p. 29 lower right: pelagic thresher shark
© Perrine Doug/Nature PL/ Jacana. p. 31 right: hammerhead © Agence Images/Iconos. p. 34 lower right: © Agence Images/Iconos. p. 35 top
left: great white shark and diver © Jeffrey Rotman/BIOS; lower right: © Alexis Rosenfeld. p. 36 lower left: great white shark © Brandon
Cole/BIOS. p. 37 top right: diver facing a lemon shark © Jeffrey Rotman/BIOS. p.40 top: finning a silk shark © Frédéric Denhez/BIOS.

# Meet the SHARK

by Catherine Vadon

MINNETONKA, MINNESOTA

# Contents

# Introducing...Sharks!

Do you think you know all about sharks? Their ferocious tempers, their thirst for blood and hunger for human flesh? Think again!

From warm tropical lagoons to the cold ocean depths, sharks have been swimming the seas for 450 million years. That's WAY longer than humans have been around. And when humans did show up, they were terrified of sharks and made up dramatic stories about their killing ways.

It was not until the 18th century that humans started to get to know sharks for who they really are. Since then, shark scientists called elasmobranchologists have identified more than 400 very different species. Some of the largest sharks are gentle giants. And even the fiercest species do not slobber over the thought of human flesh. They prefer seals, sea turtles, or smaller sharks.

Sharks hold an important place in the ocean ecosystem. Without them, the web of life would fall apart, and our oceans would never be the same. And yet these creatures are now more popular dead than alive. Humans kill more than 100 million sharks every year. They are dying faster than they can reproduce, and their numbers are shrinking. Some sharks are sold as an exotic food, while others become the ultimate fishing trophies.

What can you do to help protect sharks? Well, the best way to start is to get the facts straight. So let's take a fresh look at these amazing creatures.

# The Shark— A Marine Monster?

The shark has long been thought of as a blood-thirsty monster,
a killing machine that silently scours the seas
and snaps up carefree swimmers.

### Where Does the Word *Shark* Come From?

Until the 1700s, sharks were known as *sea dogs*. The word *shark* may have come from the German word *schurke*, or villain. Or it may come from a Mayan word for fish, *xoc*, which is pronounced "shock" or "shawk."

### The Greek Legend of Andromeda

Andromeda was an Ethiopian princess who narrowly escaped being eaten by a shark. Her mother started it all by claiming that Andromeda was more beautiful than the Nereids, or sea nymphs. The lovely nymphs were furious and asked Poseidon, the sea god, to teach the royals a lesson. Poseidon sent a sea monster—said to be a shark—to destroy the kingdom. The royals' only hope was to offer their daughter as a sacrifice. Luckily, brave Perseus came along, slayed the monster, and saved Andromeda.

## The Written Word on Sharks

The deep-sea adventure novel *20,000 Leagues Under the Sea*, written by Jules Verne in 1871, did nothing to change the shark's deadly reputation. Told from the point of view of marine biologist Pierre Aronnax, the story includes several encounters with the fierce fish: "It was a shark of enormous size advancing diagonally, his eyes on fire, and his jaws open! I was mute with horror and unable to move."

Since the 19th century, killer sharks have made newspaper headlines around the world. Sharks played a starring role in tabloids like this one, which told dramatic, hard-to-believe stories of shipwrecks and other adventures.

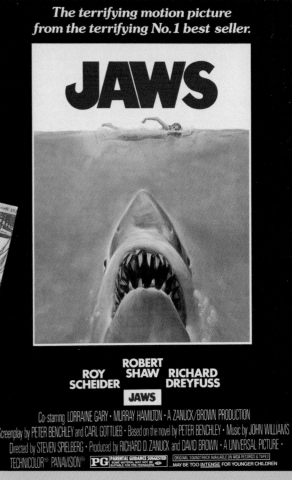

The 1975 film *Jaws* (based on a book of the same name) tells the story of a great white shark that preys on swimmers at a New England beach. The movie destroyed the sharks' reputation all over again, and many swimmers developed an unhealthy fear of shark attacks.

# Finding the Truth Behind the Tales

For centuries, few people questioned the bloody tales they heard about sharks. But over time, scientists slowly began to separate fact from fiction.

### Ancient Times

Ancient Greek scientist and philosopher Aristotle was one of the first to study sharks. Around 330 B.C., he divided fish into two groups: those with bony skeletons and those with *cartilaginous* skeletons (made of a firm but rubbery material called **cartilage**). Aristotle correctly placed sharks in the second group.

### The Renaissance

It was not until the Renaissance period—1700 years after Aristotle!—that any new scientific research was carried out on sharks. In the beautifully illustrated books common in those times, icthyologists (scientists who study fish) described different species of sharks. But their writings were still heavily influenced by wild tales and supernatural beliefs.

In the 16th century, sharks weren't the only ones with an evil reputation. A doctor and naturalist named Guillaume Rondelet wrote that women believed to be witches were sometimes called *lamiae*—a word that means both "demon" and "large shark"—because people believed they attracted and ate young men.

## The 18th Century

These were adventurous times! The king of France and other European royalty hired crews to sail the oceans looking for new species of animals. Naturalists on these expeditions collected many kinds of sharks and brought them back to be studied and sketched. Even so, scientific texts continued to reflect people's fears and misunderstandings.

## The 19th Century

During the 1800s, ocean exploration continued. And in 1872, one expedition set sail that changed science forever. For more than three years, the HMS *Challenger* sailed the world's oceans. The British crew visited all seven continents, collected thousands of samples of ocean life (including sharks), and made maps of the ocean floor. The expedition's findings became the basis of a new branch of science called oceanography.

In the past, the kings of certain Pacific islands would organize fights between men and sharks. Trapped in a shallow bay surrounded by low walls, the human contestants had only one weapon to protect them: a dagger lined with shark teeth.

# Sharks as Gods

While many people in Europe and the Americas feared sharks, some Pacific Islanders respected and even worshipped them for their beauty and strength.

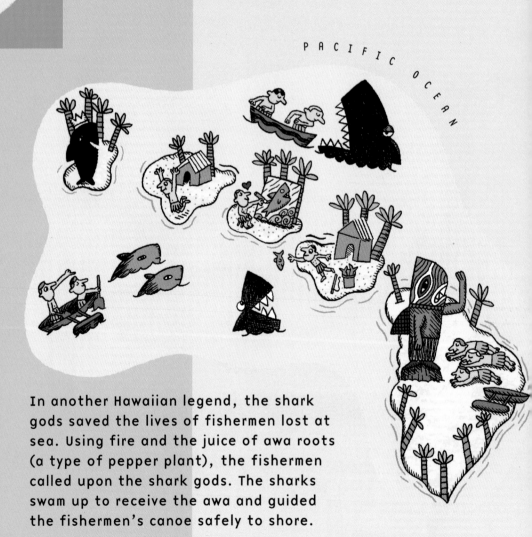

PACIFIC OCEAN

## The Hawaiian Islands

At one time, people of Hawaii believed that each of the islands had its own shark god. These gods answered to the powerful and respected Kam-Hoa-Lii. The shark king's amazing magical powers allowed him to change into a human being and to control the sea and the winds.

In another Hawaiian legend, the shark gods saved the lives of fishermen lost at sea. Using fire and the juice of awa roots (a type of pepper plant), the fishermen called upon the shark gods. The sharks swam up to receive the awa and guided the fishermen's canoe safely to shore.

"I am a shark. I won't give up a single inch of my kingdom." This was the motto of King Gbehanzin, the last king of Dohomey, a kingdom in what is now the African country of Benin. This wooden statue shows the king as a man-shark. Made during the king's reign in the late 1800s, the statue measures 63 inches (160 cm) tall.

## Solomon Islands

Another legend of a shark rescue comes from the Solomon Islands. A man was sailing a canoe between Hele and Vangunu islands when a sudden gust of wind came up. Huge waves caused the canoe to sink. The man thought that his time had come, but a passing shark let him grab hold of its fin and towed him back to land. Sharks have been a friend to Solomon Islanders ever since.

PACIFIC OCEAN

## Africa

Shipbuilders sometimes apply hammerhead shark oil to the hull of their new boats. They believe that it will bring them luck.

Fishermen from the South Pacific island of Vanuatu used shark teeth as charms to protect their small boats.

# Shark Ancestors

The oldest shark fossils date back more than 450 million years!
That's almost twice as old as the first dinosaurs. Prehistoric humans
came on the scene just 4 million years ago.

## The Golden Age of Sharks

Although sharks had already been around about 100 million years, they hit their peak about 354 million years ago. Large numbers of many kinds of sharks swam in both oceans and freshwater. Scientists think sharks may have represented 60% of all fish species alive at the time. Nowadays, only about 4% of all fish species are sharks.

**Great white shark**

*Cladoselache*

*Stethacanthus*

## Funky Fossils

Scientists have found some strange shark fossils that are unlike any species alive today. One of the oldest is the *Cladoselache*. Measuring up to 6 feet (2 m) long, it was a dreadful predator. Its body and fins were shaped for speed, and it sported two sharp spines on its back. The *Stethacanthus* was a small shark with two patches of jagged scales, one on its head and the other on the end of a strange, knobby fin. How weird is that?

## The Big One

The megalodon (meaning "big teeth") appeared about 20 million years ago. Measuring up to 50 feet (15 m) long and weighing 22 tons (20 t), it was the largest predatory, or hunting, shark that ever lived. The biggest great white sharks alive today are no more than 23 feet (7 m) long. Scientists' knowledge of the megalodon is based entirely on fossilized teeth, which measure a whopping 7 inches (18 cm) long. But we do not know much about how it lived.

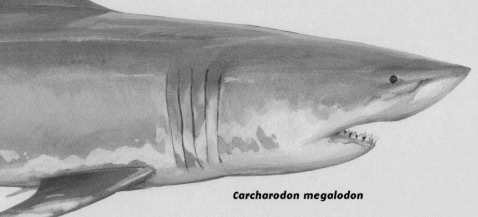

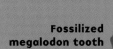

*Carcharodon megalodon*

**Fossilized megalodon tooth**

**Tooth of the modern great white shark**

### A MYSTERY IN STONE

The fossilized teeth of the megalodon were so large that, until the 18th century, people made no connection between them and the teeth of modern-day sharks. One popular belief was that they fell from the sky during lunar eclipses. Later, people began to think that the teeth were the tongues of snakes that had been turned to stone. This is where they got the name *glossopetrae*, Greek for "stone tongues." People believed glossopetrae had magical healing powers.

## EVIDENCE OF ANCIENT SHARKS

❶ When a shark died, its body fell to the bottom of the ocean.

❷ Little by little, heavy layers of sand and rock settled on top of it. Underneath, the flesh and cartilage decomposed, or rotted away. Only rarely did the body leave an imprint or outline in the rock.

❸ Often only the shark's hard teeth were preserved. In fact, because sharks lose teeth throughout their lives, finding shark teeth—both ancient and modern—is fairly common. Scientists study the shape and size for clues to ancient species.

# A Close Look at Sharks

Shark skeletons are made of a rubbery material called cartilage. (For a sample, feel the tip of your nose or your earlobe!) This sets them apart from the majority of modern fish, which have bony skeletons.

A shark's spine extends into the upper part of the tail, or **caudal fin.**

The fins on the top of a shark's body are called **dorsal fins.** The side fins are called **pectoral fins.** A pair of **pelvic fins** and, in some species, an **anal fin** are located on the shark's underside.

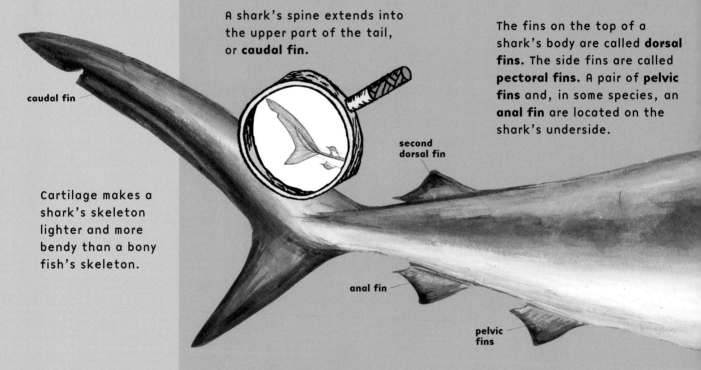

caudal fin

Cartilage makes a shark's skeleton lighter and more bendy than a bony fish's skeleton.

second dorsal fin

anal fin

pelvic fins

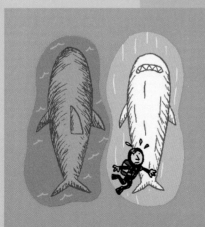

Sharks that swim near the surface, such as the great white shark and the blue shark, sport a color pattern called **countershading.** Viewed from above, their backs are the same blue-gray color as the deep water below. Viewed from below, their white bellies blend in with the light from the sky.

The liver of a shark is very large, and it contains oils that are lighter than water. This helps a shark to stay afloat.

Run your hand over a shark from head to tail, and its skin feels smooth. But run your hand the other way, and it feels like sandpaper! This roughness comes from millions of tiny spikes called **denticles** that are rooted in the skin and curve toward the shark's tail.

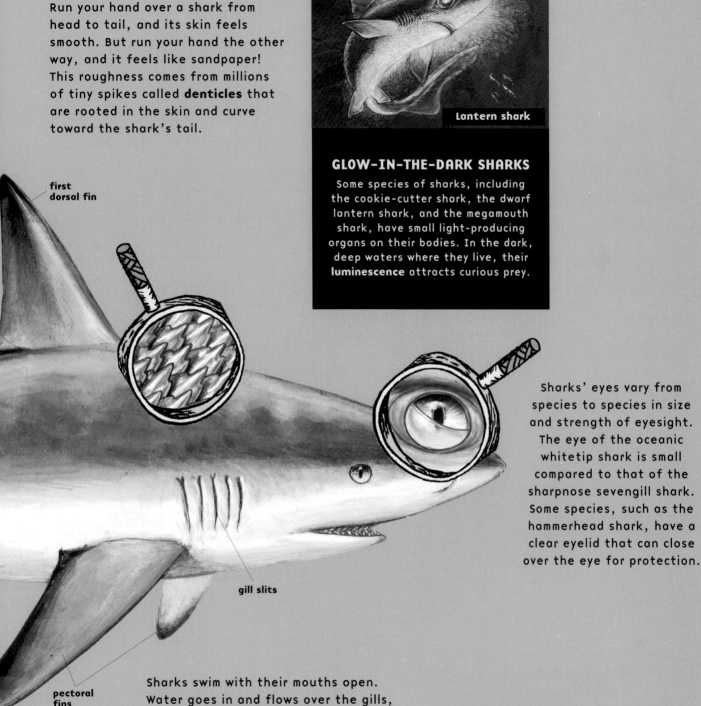

**Lantern shark**

### GLOW-IN-THE-DARK SHARKS
Some species of sharks, including the cookie-cutter shark, the dwarf lantern shark, and the megamouth shark, have small light-producing organs on their bodies. In the dark, deep waters where they live, their **luminescence** attracts curious prey.

**first dorsal fin**

Sharks' eyes vary from species to species in size and strength of eyesight. The eye of the oceanic whitetip shark is small compared to that of the sharpnose sevengill shark. Some species, such as the hammerhead shark, have a clear eyelid that can close over the eye for protection.

**gill slits**

**pectoral fins**

Sharks swim with their mouths open. Water goes in and flows over the gills, which remove oxygen from the water and send it into the bloodstream. The water exits through five to seven **gill slits** on either side of the shark's head. Most sharks have to keep moving all the time so that they have a steady intake of oxygen.

Some sharks have a stomach that can turn inside out! If one of these sharks swallows an object that it can't digest, it can push its stomach out through its mouth, rinse away the contents, and then pull it back inside.

# Putting Sharks in Order

There are around 470 species of sharks, all with different shapes, sizes, and lifestyles. New species are still being discovered, especially in the deepest oceans. To keep the species straight, scientists have sorted them into eight large groups called orders. Each order has a very long scientific name, but their common names are easier to remember.

The snouts of **sawsharks** (Order Pristiophoriformes) are long and flat, with two feelers called **barbels** and needle-like teeth. These sharks may use their snouts to slash at fish and other prey.

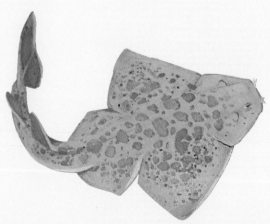

The **angel sharks** (Order Squatiniformes) hide under the sand and dart out when their prey comes near. Their huge, flat pectoral fins look like wings.

**Ground sharks** (Order Carcharhiniformes) are the largest order of sharks. They range in size from small, shellfish-chomping catsharks to large hunters such as hammerheads, tiger sharks, and blue sharks.

**Frill sharks, sixgill, and sevengill sharks** (Order Hexanchiformes) live in deep water throughout the world. They don't all look alike, but they all have either six or seven gill slits on each side of their head.

The small, stocky **bullhead sharks** (Order Heterodontiformes) use their hard back teeth to eat snails, shrimp, starfish, and other crunchy critters. They are the only sharks with poisonous spines on their dorsal and anal fins.

**Carpet sharks** (Order Orectolobiformes) have flattened bodies and stubby snouts. The huge whale shark is part of this order. Many other species in this group, such as the wobbegong, have spotted skin and fringe-like barbels. This helps them hide on the ocean floor while they wait for their prey.

The **mackerel sharks** (Order Lamniformes) include many of the great predators: white, mako, thresher, and sand tiger sharks. They have pointed snouts and jaws that extend back beyond the eyes. The name "mackerel sharks" comes from the fact that these hungry hunters are often seen around schools of fish called mackerel.

**Dogfish sharks** (Order Squaliformes) have members that live in all the world's oceans, and from the surface down to great depths. They have round bodies, long snouts, and two dorsal fins. Some have spines on their dorsal fins, and many—like the cookie-cutter shark—have sharp cutting teeth.

# Shark Record-Holders

## How Low Can You Go?

Some sharks, like the **whale shark,** live on the surface. Others, like the **goblin shark,** prefer deeper waters. But the **Portuguese dogfish shark** holds the record for deepest dweller. It can survive at depths of 11,800 feet (3,600 m).

## Going the Distance

When it comes to miles traveled, the **blue shark** beats them all. It may log 15,000 miles (25,000 km) each year as it **migrates.**

## Crowd Control

A lot of different shark species are known to gather in groups, or schools. The prize for the biggest group of all goes to the **shortnose spurdogs.** They have been seen in schools of more than 1,500.

## Sizing Them Up

Check out this lineup of sharp-dressed sharks, from the tiny spined pygmy shark to the massive whale shark.

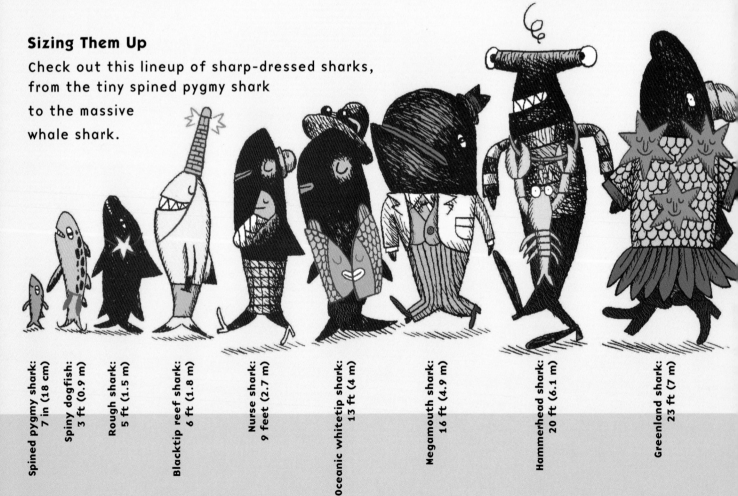

Spined pygmy shark: 7 in (18 cm)

Spiny dogfish: 3 ft (0.9 m)

Rough shark: 5 ft (1.5 m)

Blacktip reef shark: 6 ft (1.8 m)

Nurse shark: 9 feet (2.7 m)

Oceanic whitetip shark: 13 ft (4 m)

Megamouth shark: 16 ft (4.9 m)

Hammerhead shark: 20 ft (6.1 m)

Greenland shark: 23 ft (7 m)

## Old-Timer

Most sharks live for 20 to 30 years, and a few reach 80. But the Old-Timer Award goes to the **whale shark.** Experts think it can live up to 150 years, making it one of the longest-lived animals on the planet.

The **basking shark** and the **whale shark** are the two biggest species of fish in the world. They are big enough to swallow a human, but they eat only **plankton.** Phew!

Tiger shark:
24 ft (7.3 m)

Great white shark:
23 ft (7 m)

Basking shark:
52 ft (15.8 m)

Whale shark:
59 ft (18 m)

# Friends . . .

### The Pilot Fish

This striped fish is known for hanging out around sharks. By staying close, a pilot fish hopes to snap up some tasty leftovers from the shark's next meal. Whether the shark gains anything from this "friendship" is unlikely, but it doesn't seem bothered by the little fish either.

### The Remora

Remoras are the ocean's hitch-hikers. With a suction disc on its head, a **remora** attaches itself to the body of a shark—or a sea turtle or whale—and rides with its host for its entire life. Remoras snap up the leftovers from a shark's meals, and return the favor by eating any parasites on the shark's skin.

# . . . and Family

## Rays

These strange cartilaginous fish look like flattened sharks. Their gills and mouth are on their underside, and their eyes are on top. Their large pectoral fins give their bodies a diamond shape.

Some rays, like the short-nosed electric ray, are as small as a human hand, with a short, stubby tail. The largest, the manta ray, is shown here. It can grow to be 26 feet (8 m) across. The two knobs on its head help funnel plankton into its mouth as it swims.

Many rays have a poisonous stinger or sharp spines at the end of their tail. Others use their tail like a whip to slash at an enemy. And most shocking are those that can deliver a jolt of electricity.

## Chimaeras

A bird's beak, a fish's body, a ratlike tail. . . . There's something for everyone to love! In fact, chimaeras are closely related to sharks and rays. Most species of chimaeras (also called ratfish) live near the ocean floor, where they eat crustaceans and smaller fish.

So how does a shark bite its prey when its mouth is tucked under its snout like this? Well, unlike you and me, it has an upper jaw that is not connected to its skull. It can move independently.

When a shark opens its mouth to bite its prey, it pushes its jaw forward and scrunches up its snout.

With its mouth in this forward position, it chomps down. It shakes furiously back and forth as its sharp teeth saw through its victim.

# Open Wide!

Sharks' teeth come in all different shapes and sizes, depending on what kind of food they eat. The teeth grow in rows around the shark's jaw. When a shark breaks a tooth (which is pretty often), a new one from behind moves forward to replace it. Sharks' teeth never stop growing.

In **lemon sharks**, each tooth is replaced after 15 to 20 days.

The little **cookie-cutter shark** is known for its unique attacks on bigger sharks, dolphins, and seals. It seals its lips on to the victim's body and then twists itself around. Its sharp teeth carve out an oval-shaped piece of flesh as it if were cookie dough.

**Hammerhead sharks** love to feast on rays. It's not uncommon for one of these huge sharks to have stingray stingers stuck in its jaws and head.

The long, narrow teeth of the **sand tiger shark** are not used for cutting. Instead, the sharp points snag and hold onto fish, squid, and other small, slippery prey.

The **basking shark** swims slowly near the water's surface with its jaws wide open. As much as 2,000 tons (1,800 t) of water per hour flows into its mouth and out its gill slits. Plankton in the water gets trapped in its bristly **gill rakers** and then swallowed. The basking shark's stomach can hold a whopping 1,100 pounds (500 kg) of food. The basking shark sheds its gill rakers in the winter and grows new ones in the spring.

The **tiger shark** has sharp cutting teeth that can easily grind through a sea turtle—shell and all! It's not picky, though. It will eat almost anything: jellyfish, seagulls, sea lions, and even soda cans and plastic bottles.

The snout of the **Port Jackson shark** has pointed teeth in the front for grabbing prey. Large, flat teeth on the sides are good for crushing the hard shells of oysters, snails, crabs, and other shellfish.

One or two dorsal fins keep the shark upright. The caudal fin pushes it forward.

Dorsal fin

Caudal fin

A shark's pectoral fins are large and rigid. They keep the shark's body level in the water and help it to change direction and slow down.

Pectoral fin

Sharks have a pair of small fins called pelvic fins on the underside of the body, between the pectoral fins and the tail. Some species also have a single fin just in front of the tail called an anal fin. These fins all help steady the shark.

# What's a Body to Do?

Each type of shark has a body and a swimming style that match its lifestyle, whether it is a speedy hunter, a plankton gulper, or a bottom feeder.

## Feel the Heat

**Porbeagle sharks** live in the freezing waters of the North Atlantic Ocean. But that doesn't slow them down! When porbeagles swim, their muscles produce heat that spreads throughout their body. As a result, their bodies may be as much as 18 degrees F (10° C) warmer than the water.

## The Circle of Death

When food is involved, sharks don't hang back and wait for an invitation. Some species, like the **blue shark** and the **oceanic whitetip shark**, stake out their prey by swimming in circles around them. The circles get smaller and smaller until the shark senses that the time is right to attack. If another shark gets in the way, be ready for a fight!

## Feeding Frenzy

A large school of fish plus a large number of sharks equals trouble! The sharks get so worked up as they lunge for food that they create what scientists call a feeding frenzy. They bite everything in their path, including each other.

## Full Speed Ahead

The world's fastest sharks have three features in common: a torpedo-shaped body, a pointed snout, and a tail that is nearly symmetrical (the same on the top and bottom). The **great white shark** can swim an average of 2 miles per hour (3 kph)—pretty fast for a fish. But the fastest shark is the **mako shark.** It can zip through the water at more than 16 miles per hour (25 kph).

The **tiger shark** uses quick, tight turns to catch its prey by surprise.

The very long tail of the **thresher shark** gives it extraordinary strength when swimming and is used as a weapon to hit schools of fish.

# Shark Senses

Sharks have an incredible ability to detect their prey, whether it's close by or miles away. Here's how they do it.

## Cat Eyes

Sharks have a mirror-like layer in the back of their eyes, just like cats do. This boosts the amount of light that the eye senses and allows sharks to see very well in the dark. Sharks that live in deeper, darker waters tend to have bigger eyes than those that live near the surface.

## A Unique Tool

In addition to the five human senses, a shark has a few extras. One is the ability to sense weak electrical charges given off by other animals—even those that are hidden. To do this, a shark's snout is equipped with jelly-filled canals called the **ampullae of Lorenzini.** These organs also sense slight changes in water temperature (which can help guide a shark to food). The ampullae may also work with the Earth's magnetic field to help sharks find their way during migration.

## Scent-sational

Like a dog on a scent trail, a shark is able to follow a scent through ocean water and find its source. Scientists think some sharks can smell one drop of blood in 25 gallons (95 l) of water. But a shark's other senses can be just as helpful in finding food.

When swimming, the hammerhead shark swings its head from side to side. This gives the shark a better chance of seeing, smelling, and sensing the electrical charges or movements of its prey.

## Listen Up

In the water, sounds travel five times faster than in the air. Although it doesn't look as if sharks have ears, they do have organs inside their heads that pick up these sounds.

A shark's ears work closely with another sensing organ that runs down the sides of its body.

The **lateral line** is a system of fluid-filled tubes that detect vibrations in the water, such as those of a struggling fish.

## Have a Taste

A shark's mouth and throat are lined with taste buds. A bad taste may be why sharks sometimes start to eat something and then spit it out.

# How Are Baby Sharks Born?

This is a complicated question! There are actually three different ways sharks are born, depending on the species. Compared to bony fish, all species of sharks have a fairly small number of babies at a time—usually 2 to 20, and rarely more than 100.

In **oviparous** species, like the **horn shark** and the **swell shark,** females lay eggs with a tough, leathery covering. The babies grow inside the eggs and feed on a yellowish yolk sac similar to the yolk of a bird's egg.

Some eggs look like small purses and are attached to plants to keep them from floating away.

Other eggs are shaped like corkscrews and are planted in the sand.

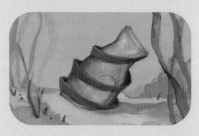

After several months, a baby shark called a pup breaks out of its egg and swims away.

In **viviparous** species, including **hammerheads** and **blue sharks,** the pups grow inside their mother and draw their nourishment from her body, as mammals do.

Most viviparous sharks are born tail-first. The pups are able to take care of themselves, and they steer clear of adult sharks, which might eat them.

A female shark may carry her young for as little as two months or as long as two years!

In the third group, **ovoviviparous** sharks, the pups develop and hatch out of eggs while still inside their mother's body. These sharks tend to be much larger at the time of birth than oviparous and viviparous species.

## Baby Cannibal

Some ovoviviparous sharks, such as **sand tiger sharks**, are cannibals (individuals that eat their own kind)! Once the hatchling pups have eaten what's left of their yolk sacs, they begin to eat their smaller siblings until only the biggest and strongest remain.

# Observing Sharks

If you've got the gear and the training, deep-sea diving is the best way to get to know sharks. Warm, tropical waters are the most common place to observe them. But that doesn't keep divers from shivering a little, either from fear or from admiration.

### Dinner Is Served!
Some diving clubs figure the best way to a shark is through its stomach. These people use food to lure sharks in and get a closer look. This dangerous practice requires a solid knowledge of shark behavior, and the understanding that these wild animals are sometimes unpredictable.

Jacques Cousteau is probably the most famous underwater explorer. From the 1950s until his death in 1997, he filmed sharks and other ocean life and helped people understand and value their place in nature. He also invented equipment to make diving easier and safer. Many other divers, such as Australians Ron and Valerie Taylor, continue to take great risks in order to learn more about sharks.

## Behind Bars

Scientists who study sharks (and many of the photographers who took these pictures) often head underwater in strong metal cages that are attached by a cable to a boat. Sometimes sharks even attack the cages. The bars keep the divers safe, but the experience still can be quite a thrill!

## Aquariums

All around the world, aquariums offer visitors a chance to see sharks close up—without getting wet! These shark species are most often small, deep-sea sharks. Large sharks need lots of space and often cannot survive in captivity.

## Where Do They Come From? Where Do They Go?

Sharks can be difficult to study because they are always on the move. And unlike whales, which have to come to the surface to breathe, sharks can spend much of their lives in deep water and travel long distances. To understand the movements of sharks, like this basking shark, scientists attach a radio transmitter to one of its fins.

Equipment on land picks up the radio signal and gives the shark's location. Another useful tracking device stays attached to the shark for a few months and then bobs to the surface, where it sends information back to scientists by satellite.

# Sizing Up the Danger

There's no denying that sharks can be dangerous. Each year, 60 to 100 people around the world are attacked by sharks. (That's out of a world population of over 6 billion people!) Only about 10 of those attacks are deadly. Many more people die from bee stings!

## IS IT A SEAL OR A SURFER?

From a shark's point of view, a seal (a tasty meal) and a human surfer look a lot alike. Surfers attract attention when they paddle and kick on the water's surface.

## Is the Great White Shark a Man-Eater?

Though it is true that this shark is strong and aggressive, its reputation as a man-eater is exaggerated. Scientists think many "attacks" are just a great white's way of checking the person out.

Thanks!

## The Most Dangerous

Only about 30 shark species are considered dangerous to humans. Those competing for the Scariest Shark Award are the white shark, bull shark, lemon shark, hammerhead, and mako shark.

## What to Do If You Meet a Shark?

Curiosity is usually what draws a shark to a diver. It takes a look and then swims on by. But if the shark feels that its territory is threatened, it will get more aggressive. Its body language will say it all. If you're a diver, it is important to learn how to read the shark's swimming style, because that may be your only warning before an attack.

## OCEAN SAFETY TIPS

• Never dive alone.

• Stay out of the water at night and when the water is choppy.

• Do not swim with a bleeding wound.

• Do not wear shiny objects, such as jewelry, in the water.

• Never swim near seals, which are a big shark's favorite food.

• If you are fishing while in the water, take your catch to shore. Do not fish with it attached to your belt.

• If you see a large shark, calmly but quickly get out of the water.

# Shark for Sale...
## From Head to Tail

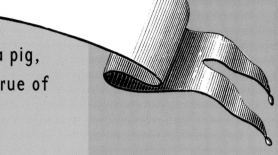

People used to say that in a pig, every part is useful. This is true of the shark, too.

Hard, rough animal skins have been used for smoothing and polishing for thousands of years. In the 1800s, people began to use shark skins. Called shagreen, these precious skins have also been used to cover jewelry boxes, furniture, and even the handles of samurai sabers.

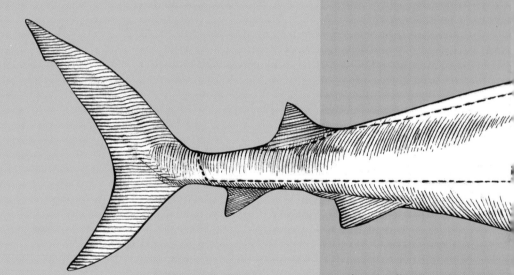

Ancient sailors made walking sticks from the vertebrae (spine bones) of sharks.

The flesh of most sharks is edible, with the exception of the **Greenland shark**. (It is poisonous, and it smells like ammonia! Yuck!) In England and Australia, the fish in "fish and chips" is often "flake," a general term for shark. The skinned meat of the dogfish shark is sold in parts of Europe as salmon, while blue shark is called "sea calf."

The fins of sharks are used to make a soup that is popular in Asia. Skinned and dried, chunks of the yellow cartilage give the soup a gooey texture.

During the 1600s in France, sharks' brains were used as a remedy for the pains of childbirth.

A shark's liver is rich in oil and vitamins A and D. One ingredient of shark liver oil, called squalene, is commonly used in beauty products and medicines.

In the South Pacific islands, shark teeth have long been attached to wood and used as weapons. Nowadays, the teeth are more commonly worn around the neck as a good-luck charm. A shark jaw may be kept as a trophy.

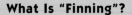

### What Is "Finning"?

Finning is the practice of cutting off the dorsal and pectoral fins of a shark and tossing the rest of the shark (which may still be alive) back into the sea. To many people, finning is seen as cruel and disrespectful, and some countries have made it illegal. But because the fins can be sold at high prices in Asia, the practice of finning continues.

Grrr!

# Sharks at Risk

With the many human activities that put sharks at risk, sharks ought to be more afraid of us than we are of them! Not only do people catch sharks for sport, but many make a living by selling the meat and fins. Now many shark species are threatened with **extinction**.

## Very Vulnerable

Sharks are more vulnerable to overfishing because they do not reproduce very quickly. Unlike bony fish, which lay thousands of eggs at a time, most sharks have fewer than 100 pups at a time. Sharks also take much longer to reach adulthood and do not reproduce as often. For example, a female great white shark must be 10 years old before she can reproduce. If she survives that long, she will be pregnant for two years before her litter of one to ten pups is born.

**Trawl fishing**

## Death to Sharks!

Many sport fishermen have high-tech equipment to help them locate fish, and some of them kill sharks just for fun. But many more sharks are killed by commercial fishermen. In **trawl fishing**, a big net is dragged along the bottom of the sea. **Gill nets** are huge nets used to catch large fish such as tuna, but any fish whose head is larger than the net holes—including large sharks—gets trapped. **Longlines** are fishing lines that can measure many miles long, with hundreds of hooks attached along their length. Longlines kill many sharks before they are old enough to reproduce.

## International Cooperation

During their migrations, sharks travel long distances and pass through the **territorial waters** of many different countries. To be able to protect sharks well, all these countries must agree and act together. In October 2004, an international group called CITES (the Convention on International Trade in Endangered Species of Wild Flora and Fauna) made trade of great white sharks illegal. And everywhere in the world, research institutes, universities, and conservation groups are making an effort to educate people and protect all species of sharks. But there is much work to be done.

# Test Your Knowledge!

**Fossilized shark teeth were once called glossopetrae.**

**True or false?**

Answer: true

**What was the maximum length of the ancient megalodon?**

– 25 feet (7.6 m)
– 50 feet (15 m)
– 100 feet (30 m)

Answer: 50 feet (15 m)

**Kam-Hoa-Lii is the name of a shark god:**

– in Africa
– in Asia
– in Hawaii

Answer: in Hawaii

**Carpet sharks got their name because:**

– they are used to cover floors
– their bodies are flat
– their denticles are fuzzy

Answer: their bodies are flat

**During its lifetime, a shark can lose:**

– dozens of teeth
– hundreds of teeth
– thousands of teeth

Answer: thousands of teeth

**How long is a spined pygmy shark?**

- 2 inches (5 cm)
- 7 inches (18 cm)
- 15 inches (38 cm)

Answer: 7 inches (18 cm)

**Which is more dangerous, the lemon shark or the megamouth?**

Answer: The lemon shark is one of just a few sharks that are known to attack people.

**How many pairs of gill slits do most sharks have?**

– 3
– 5
– 8

Answer: 5

**What is the biggest shark?**

– the whale shark
– the basking shark
– the great white shark

Answer: the whale shark

In ancient times, what did sailors make with the vertebrae of sharks?

– ashtrays
– walking sticks
– necklaces

Answer: walking sticks

During the 17th century, doctors advised people to eat the brain of sharks to:

– heal blisters
- ease pain
- become more intelligent

Answer: ease pain

How did the hammerhead shark get its name?

– because it is stupid
- because its head is hammer-shaped
- because its head is hard

Answer: because its head is hammer-shaped

Sharks have been found in waters as deep as:

– 1,000 feet (300 m)
-3,000 feet (900 m)
-10,000 feet (3,000 m) or more

Answer: 10,000 feet (3,000 m) or more

What is another name for shark meat?

– finburger
– fish sticks
– flake

Answer: flake

What doesn't the tiger shark like to eat?

– canned food
– seals
– plastic bottles

Answer: it will eat anything!

How much plankton can the stomach of a basking shark hold?

– 110 pounds (50 kg)
– 1,100 pounds (500 kg)
– 11,000 pounds (5,000 kg)

Answer: 1,100 pounds (500 kg)

What food can be prepared with sharks' fins?

– ravioli
– soup
– cake

Answer: soup

Where do we have the best chance of seeing sharks?

– in the Arctic
- in the Great Lakes
- in tropical lagoons

Answer: in tropical lagoons

# Glossary

**ampullae of Lorenzini:** tiny openings on the snouts of sharks and rays that sense weak electric charges given off by animals nearby

**anal fin:** a single small fin on the underside of a shark's body, just in front of the tail. Not all species have an anal fin.

**barbels:** thin, fleshy, whisker-like organs on the lower jaw in front of the nostrils that help some shark species taste and feel

**cartilage:** a tough, rubbery material that makes up the skeletons of sharks and rays

**caudal fin:** the tail fin of a shark

**countershading:** skin coloring that is dark on top and light underneath

**denticles:** small, tooth-like structures that make up a shark's skin

**dorsal fin:** a single fin in the middle of a shark's back that keeps the shark from rolling to the side. Some species have a second, smaller dorsal fin just in front of the tail.

**extinction:** having no living members (of a species)

**gill nets:** large, flat nets that allow a fish's head to fit through the holes but catch on the fish's gills

**gill rakers:** bristly structures in the mouths of some sharks that filter plankton from the water

**gill slits:** long, thin openings in the sides of a shark's head where small blood vessels absorb oxygen from the water

**lateral line:** fluid-filled tubes that sense small vibrations in the water and help sharks locate prey. The lateral line runs down the sides of a shark's body, under the skin.

**longlines:** fishing lines that can measure many miles (km) long, with hooks hanging down at regular intervals. Baited with small fish, these hooks are designed to catch large predatory fish, including sharks.

**luminescence:** the ability to give off light, due to chemical reactions in the body. Some sharks that live in deep, dark waters have luminous spots on their bodies to attract curious prey.

**migrate:** to move from place to place on a regular schedule, usually for feeding or breeding

**oviparous:** producing eggs that hatch outside the mother's body

**ovoviviparous:** producing eggs that hatch while still inside the mother's body

**pectoral fin:** one of a pair of fins that stick out from the sides of a shark's body. These fins help a shark steer, slow down, and stay level in the water.

**pelvic fin:** one of a pair of small fins on the underside of a shark's body, between the pectoral fins and the tail. These fins help keep a shark upright in the water. Males also use these fins to hold on to the female during mating.

**plankton:** small, floating animal and plant life

**territorial waters:** areas of ocean considered to be under a particular country's government control

**trawl fishing:** a method of fishing in which a cone-shaped net is dragged along the ocean floor, scooping up everything in its path

**viviparous:** giving birth to live young

# Index

## Learn More about Sharks

### Books:
Evert, Laura. *Sharks* (Our Wild World series). NorthWord Books for Young Readers, 2001.
Green, Jen. *Interfact Sharks*. Two-Can Publishing, 2003.
Markle, Sandra. *Great White Sharks*. Carolrhoda, 2004.
Troll, Ray. *Sharkabet: A Sea of Sharks from A to Z*. Westwinds, 2002.

### Videos:
*The Great White & The Ultimate Guide to Sharks*. Artisan Entertainment/Discovery Channel, 1996.
*Search for the Great Sharks*. Slingshot Entertainment, 2002.
*Sharks*. Nature Channel/Questar, 2004.

### Links:
Enchanted Learning
http://www.enchantedlearning.com/subjects/sharks/
Learn about all about sharks and their ancestors. A handy "Shark Dictionary" lets users look up terms and species alphabetically.

Shark School at the San Diego Natural History Museum
http://www.sdnhm.org/kids/sharks/index.html
Activities and information on sharks, with an emphasis on species commonly found along the coast of California.